123
MW01169937

Hope on Four Hooves

A true story of a military family's journey through
the struggles of PTSD

Written and illustrated by Ana B. Elise

Dedicated to:
Jamie Paxton, The Possessor of the Dream
AND
To Brave Military Kids Everywhere

Special Thanks to:
My brother, Zeke Bruck, who did a fabulous job of
editing and publishing this book

Published and printed by Ingram Spark
www.ingramspark.com
Copyright 2023 Ana B. Elise
All Rights Reserved

ISBN: 979-8-218-14790-7

Hi! My name is Ana, and I am 15 years old. This is the story of my family's Little Blessing, and how it helped our family. It began a few years ago.

From the outside, our family
appeared to be thriving. There were eight of us kids (one
more yet to come), and we would always show up at places
like concerts and parades together with Papa, Mama, and
occasionally our huge, furry Newfoundland dog, Nash.
Sundays and Wednesdays, we dressed up and drove to
church.

At Memorial Day parades, we lined up on the sidewalk to wave flags and cheer Papa as he marched, and sometimes sat afterwards listening to him speak to the crowd. People viewed us as a close-knit family.

But all those things acted as a pleasant-looking mask, covering hard times. Underneath the mask, our family was struggling.

I remember Papa speaking at one Memorial Day parade. At that time, he had served in the Army as an Engineer for about twenty-five years. He was a Chief Warrant Officer and had journeyed on many long deployments to the Middle East.

I loved seeing him in his handsome dress uniform, which he wore only for special events. It was dark blue with colorful bars, shining pins, and a matching hat that fascinated me. Papa talking of our freedom in his fancy uniform made my heart burst with pride. He was and is our hero.

At home, things were much different though. After Papa's third deployment, he started to change. He spent long hours at our family's business, and when he was home, storms would brew. He yelled a lot and got upset about many things: broken things, lost tools, messy floors, disrepair, and many other things. He especially got stirred up when someone screamed, got hurt, or made loud noises.

With eight children buzzing around everywhere like a herd of rambunctious colts, it was never quiet, and surprises never ceased. So as you can guess, there was a lot of arguments and sometimes, Papa would even break things and leave for long periods of time.

disliked that Papa was gone so much,
and when he roared, I felt like a
lost pony. I wondered why
Papa was like that.
Mama would hug me.
Once when I felt worried,
she told me that Papa
had promised never to abandon us,
and whatever happened,
God would take care of us.

Mama said that before the deployments, Papa was very funny an[d]
told jokes. She said that when he was overseas, Papa had seen a l[ot]
of horrible things, sad things, and people getting hurt. There, he ha[d]
to tote his gun everywhere because bad   people wished to kill hi[m.]

When you have experience[d]
scary things like Papa did, the[y]
do not leave you. They stic[k]
in your head like burrs in [a]
tail. Freedom isn't free, and i[t]
was costing our family dearly[.]

Like horses act when under pressure, kids will sometimes start to snap and lash out. A couple of my siblings started to behave more like aggressive stallions than brothers. One seemed to ignite trouble with Papa whenever they crossed paths, and my brother's fiery temper lengthened　　　　　　　　each argument.

Like horses, each person reacts differently to hard times. I lost some trust in people, and sometimes I dreamed such bad nightmares that I dreaded falling asleep.

Do you ever feel like just letting all your feelings gush out in bucking, rearing, and kicking as a horse would?

A few months before Papa departed for his fourth deployment overseas, Mama began driving to a farm down the road every Thursday. At the farm was an organization called Little Blessings whose purpose was to aid veterans and their families through equine (horse) therapy. Little Blessings was a vivid dream of Jamie Paxton, an Air Force veteran.

Military families experience many hardships that other families do not. First of all, the dad, mom, son, daughter, brother, or sister has to leave for lengthy periods of time; and when they do return, a taste of the bitterness of war accompanies them, and it is very difficult to readjust.

Some families have to be on the move continuously.
Many friendships both in and out of the home are damaged.
Being a veteran herself, Jamie knew of these struggles.
She wanted to help veterans, and not only them, but also their
families. Her dream was to provide help in the form of equine
assisted therapy—help on four hooves!

Why use horses for therapy? While horses can be comforting

friends, there is an even more interesting reason.

Did you know that horses sense your emotions?

They can hear your heartbeat from up

to four feet away.

Each horse is different in how it responds. Many will mimic your heartbeat, either acting contented and secure or anxious with fear, but some will attempt to comfort you when you are feeling down.

Through working with horses, people can learn to recognize and deal with their own emotions

Mama completed a fifty-week program with Little Blessings. Through it, she became more cheerful, less upset, and more able to deal with Papa's anxiety in a healthy way.

Little Blessings held programs for the grown-ups, but what about the kids? Jamie also wanted to make a special program for the military children. With lots of help and inspiration, she developed a Military Kids program. In 2020, the first group (including my four younger siblings and I) started.

Every Monday night for eighteen weeks we went and greeted other military kids, patient and caring helpers, and an equine specialist. We also met a group of the cutest, fuzziest, mini ponies ever!

Each week we enjoyed a different learning activity. Together we le
ponies around obstacles, played action-packed red-light-green-ligh
trekked across the farm on scavenger hunts, and even painted on
ponies. Each week we brushed the friendly ponies, had great fur
and sometimes got frustrated together.

Then every six weeks, we got the opportunity to ride! My little sister could not balance on the mini because she was giggling so much!

During the Military Kids nights, we learned many things. We learned to recognize our feelings, like anger and sadness, and were taught coping techniques. When angry, we learned to calm down with various things like pushing on a wall, tearing paper, or squeezing stress balls. One thing I learned was that in order to work as a team, you have to communicate as a team.

There I spent time with kids who knew what it was like to have a parent in the military so I did not need to feel so alone. I also earned to be thankful for our family because some of the kids now only had one parent. I observed that sometimes when someone is unpleasant, it is  because they have some hurt from the past. Ponies can be like that, too.

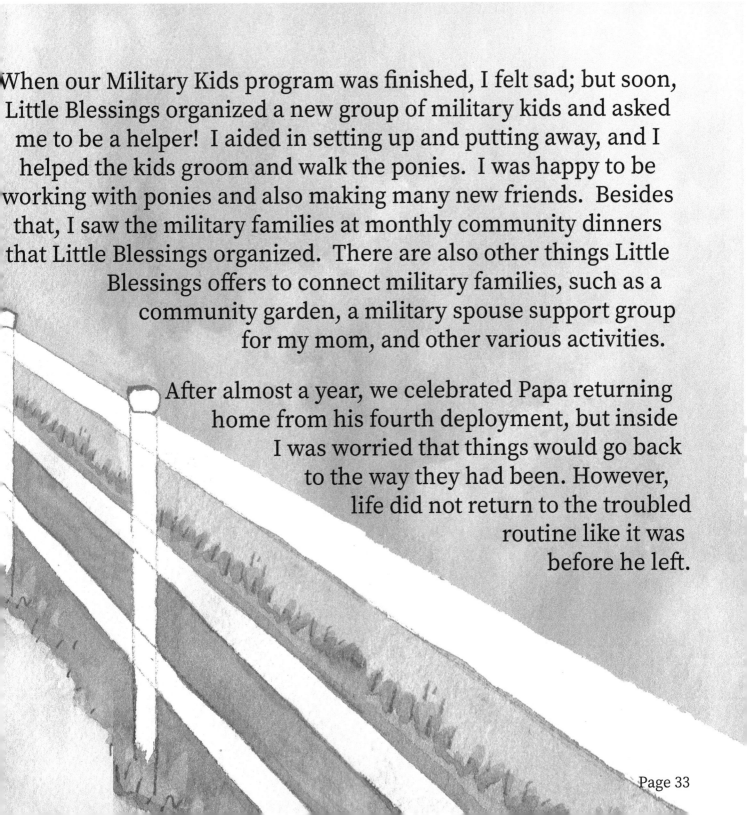

When our Military Kids program was finished, I felt sad; but soon, Little Blessings organized a new group of military kids and asked me to be a helper! I aided in setting up and putting away, and I helped the kids groom and walk the ponies. I was happy to be working with ponies and also making many new friends. Besides that, I saw the military families at monthly community dinners that Little Blessings organized. There are also other things Little Blessings offers to connect military families, such as a community garden, a military spouse support group for my mom, and other various activities.

After almost a year, we celebrated Papa returning home from his fourth deployment, but inside I was worried that things would go back to the way they had been. However, life did not return to the troubled routine like it was before he left.

Papa noticed how Mama had changed. She did not respond and get upset when he was troubled. Some of the problem kids were much calmer, too. Papa determined to spend more time with us and to try to bridle his own demon stallions. Now things are improving and getting much happier, like spring after a long winter, but this took lots of teamwork.

hortly after returning, Papa joined the Little Blessings board to try to be a support. Little Blessings was working on acquiring a new place of their own, and Papa assisted in finding a property that was formerly an old horse farm. The owners told Little Blessings that they could rent the property for $1.00 a year!

In April of 2022, Little Blessings transferred the horses they had purchased to the new ranch. Little Blessings has a big job ahead of them to renovate the property, but by working together, we can unveil the dream of giving hope to hurting veterans and their families.

We are extremely grateful to Little Blessings and so excited for that God will allow them to accomplish in the future. Little Blessings helped to slowly patch our family, healing the sorrows that were hidden deep beneath the mask. Military families will never be perfect, but session by session with the horses, Little Blessings is fighting on the home front to make them stronger.

Those around us saw the mask of a "perfect" family lined up on a sidewalk waving flags, but were unaware we were struggling. Similarly, there are military families around you who are in need. When looking from the outside, the difficulties and worries under the mask are often overlooked. I hope my story will challenge you to reach out and thank veterans for their service, and to understand better how to support veterans, spouses, and their children. On the other hand, if you are a veteran or a member of a military family who is struggling in a tough situation, remember that there is always hope. Tear off your mask and reach out for help.

Journey

Liberty

Blessing

For more information on Little Blessings Veteran Outreach:

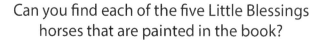

lbveteranoutreach.org

Can you find each of the five Little Blessings horses that are painted in the book?

Sonny

Tango

Jamie

*Photos courtesy of Tracy Thompson

Through the hard time my family
went through, God was with me every step
of the way. How do I know this? Because
when I was 7, I believed that Jesus, God's Son,
died to pay for my sin, and I asked Him
to be my Savior.

"That if thou shalt confess with thy
mouth the Lord Jesus Christ, and shalt
believe in thine heart that God hath raised
him from the dead, thou shalt be saved."
Romans 10:9

Now I know that he is in my heart and
will never ever leave me. One verse that has
helped me when things were rough is below:

"What time I am afraid, I will trust in thee
(God)." Psalm 56:3